Multiversal

Multiversal

poems

Amy Catanzano

Fordham University Press

New York | 2009

Library of Congress Cataloging-in-Publication Data

Catanzano, Amy.
Multiversal / Amy Catanzano. — 1st ed.
  p.   cm.
ISBN 978-0-8232-3007-5 (pbk. : alk. paper) —
ISBN 978-0-8232-3006-8 (cloth : alk. paper)
  I. Title.
PS3603.A895M85 2009
811'.6—dc22   2008047147

Printed in the United States of America
11 10 09 5 4 3 2 1   First edition

For my husband, Jeremy Lampo

Contents

Foreword | *Michael Palmer*

Ut pictura poesis. Most poetry over time has adhered, in one fashion or another, to the Horatian mimetic dictum. Of course, particularly in periods of social and spiritual turbulence, the representational model has not infrequently come into question. Whenever the "real" has been perceived as elusive, or illusional, realism itself has in turn been seen as inadequate to the poetic project. It is at this point that the aleatory, the plural, the phantasmal and the expressionistic elements of the art have gained currency. Thus the Baroque in Europe during the religious wars, and thus too the many strains of modernism and vanguardism throughout the violence and upheavals of the Twentieth Century. Amid such crises, rather than gazing into the mirror, or "holding the mirror up to nature," poets have often passed through the looking-glass into the domain of psyche, dream and counter-logicality, where "poetic logic" operates beyond the constraints of narrative unity, ordinary perception and traditional formal boundaries.

"I strive to crack and vaporize the medium . . ." So states the poet in "Objects of the Visible Language." Further along arrives the line, "shifting the glossolalia in my blood." To those ends, Amy Catanzano offers us a poetic vision of multiple orders and multiple forms, of a fluid time set loose from linearity, and an open space that is motile and multidimensional. The work exists at once in a future-past and in a variety of temporal modes. (The vision in fact is not so distant from some of the wilder implications of recent theoretical physics, to which Catanzano refers.) At one moment the scale is intimate, at another infinite. She interrogates our means of observation and measurement (the telescope, the ice-core), our mappings, our cosmic calculations, our assumptions about cause and effect. In the background, "there is a war being fought," though which of many wars, cultural, scientific, military, we are not told. In a time of displacement such as ours, she seems to say, in place of "universals" we must imagine "multiversals," in place of the fixed, the metamorphic. Immediately, however, as I write the word, I hear "play" in "displacement," and am reminded of the play, the playfulness, of poetic language, ever meant to unlock the gates of perception. In our multiple present ("this present and that one"), we await the Big Bang; in the tradition of the historical avant-gardes, we await beginnings and becomings, however ancient.

Nonetheless, as much as the frame may be cosmic (micro- or macro-), it is important to remember that the work serves the vital questions of the here-and-now, "the flowering of the world," the corrosiveness of violence, the primacy of desire, the necessity of wonder. *Multiversal* represents an effort to see things as they are through an act of poetic reimagining, that is, to see variously within the folds and fields of the actual, where the *physis*, or life force, resides. "A blaze within a tighter blaze, engulfed." "Earth pivots on a pearl."

Acknowledgments

Thank you to my husband, Jeremy Lampo, for his love, support, cover art, and the title of this volume.

Thank you to my family for their love and encouragement: Attilio and Cathy Catanzano, Patricia McCabe, Charles Catanzano, Rachel McCabe, and Holly McCabe.

Thank you to my friends and colleagues for their support.

Thank you to Michael Palmer for selecting this volume for the Poets Out Loud prize.

Thank you to Poets Out Loud Series Editor Elisabeth Frost and Fordham University Press Editorial Director Helen Tartar.

Thank you to the editors of the following literary magazines in which some of these poems first appeared:

American Letters and Commentary: "Anti-Guardian 6:7:9"
Aufgabe: "Document Mending: backdrop, singularities, document, redshift"
Bombay Gin: "Notes on the Enclosure of Shores"
can we have our ball back?: "The Ground Between Us"
Colorado Review: "Choose Your Own Adventure"
Columbia Poetry Review: "Series for Insubordination"
Conjunctions: "Notes on the Enclosure of Sums," "The Barbelith Poems"
Conjunctions on the Web: "Notes on the Enclosure of Beams," "Objects of the Visible Language"
Denver Quarterly: "The Book of Imaginary Planets," "Notes on the Enclosure of Depths," "Notes on the Enclosure of Fields"
Facture: "Document Mending: featherweight," "Notes on the Enclosure of Spheres," "Yellowstones"
Fence: "Chromatica"
A Best of Fence (reprinted, forthcoming): "Chromatica"

For Immediate Release: "Portraiture"
Morkville: "A Condition of Hyperspace"
Volt: "Notes on the Enclosure of Sparks"

The first quotation in "The Barbelith Poems" is derived from Ivan Chtcheglov (alias Gilles Ivain), "Formula for a New City," in *What Is Situationism?*, ed. Stewart Home (San Francisco: AK Press, 1996). The second and third quotations are from Grant Morrison, *The Invisibles*, vol. 2, nos. 18 and 12 (New York: Vertigo/DC Comics, 1994).

Quoted material in "Objects of the Visible Language" is from Rick Straussman, *DMT: The Spirit Molecule* (Rochester: Park Street Press, 2001).

"Flowers of Space" is based on Dōgen, "Kuge: Flowers of Space," trans. Yasuda Joshu and Anzan Hoshin. http://www.wwzc.org/translations/kuge.htm.

Multiversal

Notes on the Enclosure of Fields

My translator microbe is a singular terrain.
It ties my magic to its jungle face to face.
The moon is everything inside the dusk's
psychotropic skin. Yes, those are waves.
We pretend we feel through the dark without them.
It's in my left or right hemisphere: the wake
from the animal wing. It's why I assume, deep
in the magnetic field, that the wing exists
in my attempt to unearth it. Pressing the shore
beneath you, you are never sleeping, instead
writing "ongoing moon" in the sand
with a peeling stick. Or those dreams living
behind the eyes, listening to the derailment splash.
But there is always something to say
about how all the spots and stripes get there.

The Book of Imaginary Planets

0254.98

This is how we define change. A breath on the shoulder. From the lightest to the darkest. Chains of ultraviolets, the light should have. As space is stretching, you are thinner than a flame. Its spiral arm.

462.017

There is no outside. This is the same as asking, what does the universe look like from the outside? Is the opposite of the moon the five-pointed star? An adjustment so that your clock will be running faster than all the clocks on earth?

610.9893

Does everything fit together now? Will we be provided with an arrow of time that does not flip over? Just after the Big Bang, the universe operated in a state of low entropy. Our inner limbs. The theory that gave us the famous equation.

0137.001

The above explanation is an oversimplification. It heralded a wave of jewels, a revolution. Two faces of light, because one underpins the whole. If it exists it has to have certain properties, like you. Already out there.

365.074

Already out there. Tiny strings were vibrations of the fifth dimension. Some are aspects of just one superforce, a dent in the canvas. And so, if a piece of the phantom circle is missing, so are we.

58.9684

As it expanded it cooled. As it expanded. It was a tunnel or a landmark that rose out of normal space. It had to exist everywhere, even in the empty space of atoms, your breath.

493.0102

Now that the future is unfolding all the time you are away. It will readily absorb the light. If the wavelength is slightly changed, then the atoms, then the light. It's the one falling in who sees the clock.

1162.957

As the sunlight is passed through a prism. Which is the music for this? As it crosses the entry, then the heart. Then it crawled within the fault. Then it shone inside the door. Drunk at the moment

186.090

When the universe was the size of an orange. As one corridor explodes. As another starts to bristle. Instead we divided the trails by their trails. Down by the gold water at the end of a. At the edge of a. Shifting mission control.

304.01

Where billions and billions of windows. Where the rose around you gently pieces. Your naked shoulder. My breath. Specks of specks and broken shale. The murmur of your weightlessness. Collapsing subterranean stems.

861.589

Think of the trampoline model of space. Let us consider what it would be like. My breath on your shoulder. Now two faces of light, one like you. Formed from deep-blue disc florets and sky-blue ray florets.

379.381

Your breath on my shoulder. A warp in my heart. Beyond the band of blue is the blackness of space. From space it is the gradual transition that grips: light blue, dark blue, purple, black. A long breath.

198.0274

Stars continue to burn and shine all the time. The patterned light wanders all over. Your shoulder, that star, my breath. Any of these worlds. The more matter that is poured into a black hole the bigger it gets.

Objects of the Visible Language

Do you believe in the once indivisibility of atoms?

The arranged ruins of planetary lights?

The core of the planet was several

in the mind of the australopithecine.

Consider the astral cataloging

DNA Mad Scientist.

One million dollars sure buys a lot of simulation!

For hidden deep within the spiral code

of the imprisoned green mountain

beats the anti-solstice arsenal.

Stitch stitch the requirement if the species is to propagate.

And when the hypercube collectors go to auction . . .

        And if the eyespot locus in your palm . . .

Others choose the tropic within.

      Do you know who built that little pyramid of dreams

in your head?

          What about that quiet machine you own

that peels back the separatrix boundary

from the giant's eye?

I strive to crack and vaporize the medium, leaving behind

a replica of the route—

We are used to the converse: water and hills, apples drop.

We are often provided a formalism in which the patterns

grow

chaotic, which is non-periodic,

and when the system becomes overwhelmed with choices

the medium dissolves, repeating the route of its future

non-structure.

As if each and every grain of sand is x-rayed somewhere on the surface.

When I first saw you I ran forward

are there edges on that?

As a result, the body of evidence for gradient fields proliferated.

The arterial tree-like structure of the lungs

that didn't quite exist.

As if the world I claim—high up—does the break of symmetry

dream even there?

The hardened fire of natural opal is all color and solace and candor.

I remember the

        wood's gypsy circles

                in deep time

                        and without dimension—

Is such fluxus geology appropriate for this situation?

        Between the eye and its rock star fractal,

    straight into the future!

           Observations at no atomistic level in all one sees.

Since only by way of counterpoint can I build an invention

to measure the behavior of everything

clockwise.

Have you thought the slope to be steeper

where the periphery disconnects?

Where the clock's second hand shoots through

the heart of the star—approaching more temporal RNA, please:

shifting the glossolalia in my blood.

"They were cloaked, like silhouettes. They were glad to see me.

They indicated that they had had contact with me as an individual before.

They seemed pleased we had discovered this technology. [. . .]

I thought of how the South Pacific natives

could see only Captain Cook's

small boats, and not his big ships, until they actually climbed on board

and touched them."

Notes on the Enclosure of Cores

The ice sheet records its own
history, drilling right into
the dome peak

Its continuum veil we trace
ourselves, marking underwater
points of entry

As something like pearl
drops from the edge

Where I am always gathering
a present terrain

From a hinge inside
the shore

As I am thinking
about placement—

How there is something
to learn from an empty map
of the known universe—

Which reveals the nova, swollen
in bloom, rejecting its
point of origin in favor
of something else:

A quantum arrowhead, invisible,
loosening the lithosphere
from my eyes

Clinamen Principium

within the atomic swerve does a probability
                                        always branch?

                              presto! my lightning
            of apparitions:
                              masks depicting
                                        something else.

                              by sentences we culminate.
            the philosopher's stones
                    ingest me to astonish. I interpret the terse fires
                    but cannot go in.   I forest

                              territorializes, to think visibly
            my extensions must never be fixed—

                    a material presence, this gesture
            is a galactic
            strata made from

                    suggestion, amplitude, oracular
            nevertheless.

what is the definition of gravity, which is
                                    its snapshot?

as I crowned the perimeter
                        with words: freethinking
and someone clapped
in unison
from the velvet balcony above.

              the object of time and space, you altered
my findings, equidistant

                      like planets in a rare orbit
everywhere
you and I, our subjects
collecting
                  all of it, dear
                              space reader

please describe the borders
that multiply you, their indeterminacies,
                        the furtive
          exceptions.

in pictures of the universe, how do we keep from
                                        looking
                                              inward?

                        as if the result of the expansion is

music or the collection
            and collision of vibrating strings
                        that are encountered when we play
                                    instruments meant for reasoning.

what is the distance between light
                    and its future?

                    I point to fugitive patterns
moving the compass,
                    which is a metal
                    designed for a certain kind
                    of revolt.

for and against the senses. the war. the axis
        of directions in which we
                accumulate ourselves.

                        simultaneously, history
                    hallucinates from its sleep: you are

calibration, scavenger, superfluous
            within the war.

                    my readership is part-immaterial.

            as if each dream, or the
            experience of it,

privileges relative
                structures, the ongoing
                measure of the dream in proportion
to the dreamer.

The Barbelith Poems

10. Octopi change color as a mode of communication, and this distressed him, enormously.

09. "In their own cathedral" of shock waves, calculating not end dates but zero dates, sentencing others to a life without "everyone will live," writing *a mystery is often accompanied by its fraudulent twin* . . .

08. With weaponry we separate the fish from the fish, crusades are undone on the walls of buildings, bright blue shutters are opened to the private dome, nothing is preemptive but the elaborate luster of scrawled names, and you, tagging monuments before your adaptive fingerprints are photographed in three dimensions.

07. Pulling it apart layer by layer one can imagine how, under the banner of Neoism, they made their location: sweat and city temporarily in mid-ripple, forming watery hives in throngs, then collapsing over a luxury jurisdiction. Could the bright blue shutters have been opened when he moved away? Each page in which "real ink cloud" appeared was torn. Shimmering through to ruby blossoms, the Law of Fives is not as discordant as it used to be: sonic roses have risen where first an empire lisped.

06. Photography, as a whole, is not adequate. That I swallowed the lily is not adequate.

05. *When push comes to shove you pull on gravity for your pleasure, letting those thin discs of Beta Pictoris pleasure you.*

04. I was told to blister rather than to break. The embrace of narrow. A hook of entry. Thus nothing in common moves wings. Wings move toward nothing in common. Soon the participants perceived the neutral painting bare. We practiced something we admired. Degrees are year long under the statue of stars. We sob. Rubies burst. Speechless, and I spill my serrated heart all over town recorded for miles.

03.   "Watch for the word BARBELiTH on your walls."

"If our words are circles, theirs are bubbles."

02. The Big Bang happens only once and in the future. Not a star but a strategy of flutter. I could say it just once before astonishment took over—batteries blinking awake in micromuseums, and I, clipped by a thin tulip of air—and you changing the shapes of things—and others doing this too by singing some out from their factories. Hence, I didn't give way to astonishment, but rather observed the tetragram of troops closing in, taking note of the maneuvers they used: an accuracy I hadn't seen since words were words and entire brotherhoods could travel by mirror.

December 21, 2012

Option 01: Your human hands are what you pay for.

Option 02: This is a plume, a trick hierarchy of billions.

Option 03: This is a ghost, a noose, something on lashes.

Option 04: This is an emblem minus the moon of incident.

Option 05: This is a thorn-opal, found split in the estuary.

Option 06: This is a ring, a limb, something that floats.

Option 07: Duration left to itself bends everything red.

Option 08: This is a cubic pearl, skinned, in tropical water.

Option 09: It was a period of apologies on arrival.

Option 10: This is a vine, a lock, what we're made from.

Option 11: This is a bribe, ensuring silence, a deep slit.

Brilliantine

What do you see when you look at
the space behind your ribs?

    sunspot

                supervolcano

While farther north the area becomes
more mountainous still,

    and even farther:

the globe's underwater face, its
enduring lost city.

There is geological significance
    of my heart

on the mid-ocean ridge.

My alluvial layers end up in the sea.

We appear separated by more than
ontological distances.

Take the floral aurora

    and its UFO

           filigree

or the belief in cardinal numbers
someone else

beholds. Boundaries

    in plate tectonics
have different names under us.

When you remember the future

I become more and more
      ancient less
      tidal.

Notes on the Enclosure of Shores

dampkring

meaning *atmosphere*

requires certain stringent

things of myself

from the unseen

midst:

skywalkers

battlestars

instruments

I bequeath

to the idea of the sea:

that is, no notes at all;

rather, they

persuade

from afar

                         the tiny bells

in flight in my

      new-heart

           where, even

memories, first-out-of-the-nest

     floating over

the Alps at 30,000 feet

          until my perspective, that

          seam,

          reverses

the bird of history

disappears

through the swirls of its smudged

wings

maneuvering

my hypnosis and its Mandelbrot

sunrise

right before me like a real cosmic

trigger

(I remember that, too)

so that, in life, it's always possible

to trust those spiral

galaxies

        unwound to you, like words,

each day you've refused to map.

Chromatica

White blooms slip
Fan out their limits near the
Bathysphere

A kingdom of low-water marks

What I call *counter measure*
In relation to perspective

The study of force fields
And the closure indicated by them

    ★

As the face of a shell
Expelled on the shore
Constitutes a certain song

Fields of g-force unfold

Part wick   Part winged

Where streams of
Gene expressions
Are computationally intense

Anchored by spirals
The astronaut's spectacle
Fast-spinning collisions of
The heart with the road

    ★

This lavish show
Prying open the gates
To the city's only
Waterfall, which is

An effect of the mediated story
A deep-sea revolution
Negotiating the borders
Spreading all of its

Outer space

Between the dream's
Airy blues

★

There are still more possibilities
For the M in M-Theory

One of the islands
That was found
On the M-Theory planet
Corresponds to a theory
That lives not in 10
But in 11 dimensions

★

Where waters rush
The pathways of the
Circulatory system
And in their centers revolve

The beginning and end of
A primary expansion

Within the human breastbone

Behind our ∞ enhanced
Inner/outer eye

Notes on the Enclosure of Beams

A future character of ownership maps it.
I am squaring iron dunes
assuming each side of the solar aquarium.

Blurs a different tradition figures bend.
The translucent border mostly invented the cell and veil.
That the cell brushed away its veil. The veil looked longingly
at the winged arrow. The arrow, a blurry wing, shook its
optic cells from its claws.

Exits got larger and larger
because the world, to endure exactly down the center.

Causal, an escape from gravity.
Causal, your perfect tunnel.
Circling in the splinterhole sky.

It was majestic sweetening
the properties a little:
banishing below scenes,

multipliers of the mouth to mouth.
Darwin centers of the brain play reenactments,
a comedy gearshift

accidental myself among them a head of eyes:
wiring whose mission prevents
prevalent laws from advancing,

rejecting all context for the space
of appearance—absent, unaccounted for, a flourishing.

Flowers of Space

When five petals open a single flower
       at the moment when
               the flower blooms,
and the time and place of the opening
reveal sparks and flames of the blue lotus,
or the time and place of the blooming
is a single spark
       and hundreds of blue
lotuses blooming in the sky, blooming
on the earth,
       blooming in the past, blooming
in the present, we are seeing
       the blue lotus
flower within fire, where the blue lotus
       blooms, so that we know
               the fire within.
When the flower blooms the world arises.

Spring and autumn flower and fruit trees
       of gold, which all have flowers
and fruit,
where human trees have flowers, where
       human flowers have flowers
       and withered
trees have flowers, and the flowers of space
are known through the blossoming
and falling of flowers in the sky,
       of flowers on the ground,
through the realization
of the blossoming and falling
       of the flowering of the world,
         and are the vehicle
       through which we travel,

these flowers of space, and which are
seen by those with clouded eyes who,
            in the wake
                        of the eye
                                    of reality,
know that space is originally with flowers.

The act of raising a flower and blinking
is a manifestation of flowers of space,
and the eye of reality is called
                        clouded eyes
and *flowers of space*,
                        and awakening
and the body of reality are just two petals
opened by this flower of space.
Through meeting one with clouded eyes,
        we can understand flowers
in space, see flowers in
space, and then see flowers in space vanish,
                for clouded eyes exist
        because of flowers of space,
        and there are many kinds of space
and many kinds of flowers, including cloudy
flowers and space that is a single grass.

We should take a panoramic view,
        for flowers have never appeared,
            never arisen,
                    never vanished,
flowers have never been flowers,
        space has never been space,
and space flowers

give forth space fruit and drop space seeds,
and since what we perceive
                    are the five petals
opening the flowers of space, we should see
the flower form of all things,
since anything
that can be imagined is a flower and fruit
of space.
            If there is a single cloud in the eye,
flowers in the sky
            will tumble in all directions.

Notes on the Enclosure of Sparks

Deep waves are invisible.

White beach knots the glass.

How many rush to the bright outline?

Step forth from its splayed shoots?

Was once spring off that mountain.

Someone will say, marigolds slip through rushing.

Forming droplets.

Stained glass blue of an underwater world.

Between the green and starship.

Know this.

A long departure where blossoms.

The micron planet.

Such as the glow of altered fields.

The city was crowned with expansive borders.

It was called a spin-exchange.

The inconsistency of impetus.

Parallel flutter of falling leaves, a water mist.

When the body's entry initiates contact.

An army of self-assembly.

Wing of biomimicry.

Made of marble or mirror, birch or brush.

A solar cell inspired by a leaf.

Let's say a particular view of spectrum, a theory of vanishing.

With a roadmap for refueling.

With the field flowers spraying their plasmas inward.

Hitting the purple fold of the bright field.

The burning false edge.

Document Mending

featherweight.

, left to the left edge. A vale
suspended. A wheel turning or not. As is
didn't recede,

didn't whisper the rules quite
right

backdrop.

From the room—constructed, elaborate, in folds—
the wave, too, has had its gestures solved
in the wind: an hour, a character, uprooted. And yet
a letter has closed. A shade
has fallen back on its slumber. And then the moment

becomes a mirror at my feet, its wash
torn with light—an unhinged
wire orbiting its own equation. Or was it a face, a fleck
of water, a hair singed by the lens,

so now the room becomes electric, thrown clear?—

singularities.

A blaze within a tighter blaze, engulfed.
Scarlet poppies bloom, or blue nights—
and people, too, just beyond their
peripheries.

document.

Looking backwards at something,
all that can be recollected is the
single motion of moving forward
or backward too quickly. A loss,
however infinite.

redshift.

With precision a calendar, the machine.

There is a should be. There is a rotation. There is a noticeable place. Or forever.

That the beginning will be like an evening tucked so tightly into itself that when it's released back into daytime at dawn, it will tear—

Notes on the Enclosure of Waves

The syzygy wavers gold like roads in dry heat.

There is no path, words

have futures, aerial
compounds

undersea.

Since then I have not quite lived the same.

Someone is leading the paradox to its wayward conclusion. Compared to a clock in flux in the attic, we are both meter and metric. With even more momentum I have passed through the page timelike yet moonlight.

Assemblage views are spreading.

But to the idea of the observer we are always relative by definition. Distances are governed by another set of behaviors:

We vow
With maps
That fall
To the sky
Our roots
Releasing
The alpha
Chapters

Through
Circles or
Echoes.
Will this
Victory
Be poised or
Marked
Like an
Exploding
Star?

We feel a tremor and flower. In islands. In acreage. Surrounds the vessel like an airlock for the eyes.

     Earlier I devised a system for decompression. The light lasts for hours and alters. High cliffs tower on the ocean floor in mutual benefit. The ship above the ocean sang something as it ascended.

Your voice like a vector assembles the mechanics.

Some will be made from   flaws or

                                prisms

in the ecosystem:

                The atmosphere cupping
                    inward like the petals
                        of an interlocking rose

Cut this. Into ribbons. As we swim. You sing. Thread the ribbons. Through the sea:

> Propelled
> By
> Homophone
> Through
> Diurnal
> Solutions
> Under the
> Wing
> The world
> Releases us
> In trails the
> Far skyline
> Incites—

Embracing, we seek charms.
There is a colony of wings at the bottom of the ocean.

The plants dance underwater. The sea's
Connective tissue.

As if one letter is suppressed
And the rest waver.

Conversely, we narrate the code until something
Floats.

Under the sea
We

Grow stronger.

The code emerges through the surface as a
Watermark.

Envisioning its lacy borders.

It has reasons to interact.

I respond autobiographically to the evolving cinema:

We are proof of

                                        The constellations
                                        Reflected in the sea
                                        At nightly
                                        Intervals, brightly
                                        Visible like crests
                                        Always gathering

            What is
            That
            Moon in the
            Mind I
            Want to
            Split?

What does
It take
To see the
Inner
Rings?
Can full
Moons
Still tell
Time? I
Measure
Myself
Against
Unfamiliar
Clouds:

Dreaming
In extreme
Geographies
Something
Is located
Under the sea
Breathing
Immaculate
Nowhere
Waves into
Me

The Ground Between Us

a measure of our solar

system in blush

our spatial reasoning

pressing toward

the gravel mountain without

the abundance of green

to extend us

nevertheless the wave

of entanglement

our part on the log bridge

inventing crowds

I find I think of you

in closer

the story of the starlings

around you

as if my calculation

describes a pulsar's

endpoint despite this

discussion of polarity

rays branching

the black from the bark

in the phase diagram of the sun

reveals the exaggeration

of breathing

within us

fringe, spare, tremor

one star light-years

from another

my version of the

everywhere equator

I was

thinking

the animate leaves

upon the current expedition

which held in their spark

a field of globe flowers

shimmering outside the eye

for as long as possible

as we unfold
one petal after the other
dethroning borders
the four directions
simultaneously inside
the earth

Notes on the Enclosure of Spans

The sky is no door.　　　　It is a transfusion　　　　of places,

like headstones　　　　or the moon.　　But the pellicle's　　　too blue.

The sun will　　　　rise and fall　　　as though in the sea.

At the ceremony of　　　　infinite　　　　territory

one light-year　　　any panorama　　　is equal to or greater than.

Composition　　invalidates　　the control　　　　in the experiment.

Your tests　　　like my tests　　　group by　　　becoming.

We construct　　　　a temporary　　　　architecture.

I calculate no　　　　sudden contour.　　　To the outlaw

borealis, frozen　　in its　　　　necessary language,

this is the spiral　　　alloy　　　of homecoming.

Under the Perils

At last the nightlong row of saturated bark, near hills through the pale you seek something, offer me my own city. It happened all at once: pools and ice. The curve of pools within the ice. Ice breaking around the pool. Water floats. Holding your breath all the way back, the so-called margins of error, no time, having dreamt it only speech.

It is our understanding that I am working as much as possible. The dancers left the house limping. The fruit was all the same color. I see two people trade mouthpieces. They claim they are survivors of the miracles. In the vaulted morning, at the two-way mirror flashing indigo, I lose the myth of the witch and the eagle. The famed belt of satellites. I speak of this persistently for the shrill of high-tide warnings. From which of the four translucent regions do I bury marked sand dollars out to sea.

Gathered at the foreground, around signs near the heartwood, near the theater showing *Starlight in Two Million*. The orchestra is aligned. The instruments, tuned. The premise is as clear as texture welling up in the folds of leaves. It could be called beauty or behavior. As if contained in the temporal bone, the time through which a portion of your heart extends. Sunlight empties the body of all its transparencies, leaving space for a rocket and its gemstone engine. Earth pivots on a pearl.

roy g. biv, there is a war being fought, but I heard the trick is to dismantle all sides. So I divide the glow from the gold. The ricochet culture from the resistance to it. The dreams from the asteroid threats that race within me. But there are rooms containing all of this. I was 945,388,800 seconds old, creating space charts *a posteriori*. The elements are not worth memorizing. Careful what you breathe, molotov-singer. A benevolent person stands by as a reminder. What drilled in as it lit.

Anti-Guardian 6:7:9

Dear Evasive Precaution:
The exaggerated tips of flapping tendrils gave the illusion of light speed, if only briefly.
Our proof of species epidemic. Indeed, the yellow gallery light of the honeycomb,
and the gaps not gaps at all. Was perhaps a thing you saw, circling, was on the other
side of the nearest street, calling itself a heliport then a firmament, at full stature on
the neck of the land, blinded by its own advantageous circuits, the boulevard exit
scene ethically repeated until death.

Dear Successive Square Levels,
a) The telescope is a time machine.
b) A blue sky makes a red sunset.
c) My lionheart: see *Evasive Precaution*.

To: A Single Ocean Collapsing Over and Over
From: Collecting for the Syntactical Harvest

with and, of, 54
Bird of Joy, 12
the bystander, 8
caryatid of the universe, 5
a devourer, 44
playing cards, 19
by the wood, 56
our marionettes, 51
the color of capsules, 30
International Flag Code, 2
coiled around, 6
little fossil bones, 9

too electromotive, 1
from the hook, 20
to quickly nullify, 31
on the floor, 53
recurrent piracy, 5
a scarred tongue, 34
the pocket watch, 11
secret societies, 23
our brickwork, 46
interlaced with, 2
V for victory, 33
finely crisscrossed, 9

the candied water, 36
is so innocuous, 7
her first globe thistle, 58
lever casting, 13
rockbottom, 14
with embrasures, 26
shell-pocked, 25
the fugitive stirs, 22
our human crews, 15
burnished ruts, 10
my dazzling warrior, 18
beneath soluble skin, 30

Dear Sudden Camouflage:
What pushed us toward the pattern
With such focus, such affliction?

A sun's disappearance
Yet without toxic spires
Yellow flares
Consistency damage

The atmosphere was stronger
Galaxies are known to move
Away from one another
Central nuclear regions
Become smaller while the galactic
Arms become wider
More open

Dear Enter (a Country, etc.):
When I approached you, you resisted, we fought, you hid from me, I found you,
you became nervous, I threatened you, you made excuses, you walked away, I had
to follow: the arrow of mica, because I made a map _____ false color in the air
shows up as blue; a crescent unit of genetic code _____ cloaked
blueprints of the reliquary; for the distribution of dramatic events _____
often with overlapping explosions of fluorescent edges burning cusps in the
tracery _____ is not an answer to: so bluish: took samples (of the bluish
_____) and half the days devoted to the breadth of its blue, blue outline.

Dear Negotiator, at any Point:
The relation between freedom and deep space depends on this.

Notes on the Enclosure of Spheres

If a note of music is the foundation for using a voice
the way a makeshift window uses a sky, then the voice must
contain some liquid flicker, some mist, some that is never
shaped.

The dawn inserted. I took my hand and kept speaking
of reasons. But something important was on fire.
Close to your chin where I was looking was this thing,
a patch; I couldn't tell whether it was for an eye or a shirt.

Dear Developer
Dear Discovery
Dear Rosewood

duplicated, you are nearly the same as you are now: a
ripple in water past the outward edge of land, tracing its
own roots. I am the grid of my face: close up
and slightly jeweled.

Dear Dinosaur
Dear Intersection
Dear Orderly

licking the butterfly knife under the orange tree.
This is the part that trespasses from the outside.

I resume the lurching forward and arrange myself.
You will have slow-motions while my eyelids are
pressed together repeatedly for the span of a year.

Clearly, the rite of passage slipped from the cap of the
eye. It was a fiction if not a business that withstood.
Time and scope of many virtual songs poured through
a gleaming white net.

Telephone jungles ran deep among identical waves.
Before there was sandstone there were sandstone
machines.

Beyond the cloth doll living real, you bring me
one so I am able to fray its ember.

Rut plus red gem. Gems like human hooks. Darts
like dark matter occupy fragile eyefuls. And when I
speak your name, do you inhabit precisely there?

though to liberty
everything lunatic can happen

Like afterthoughts, the trees behind
us shook. Not the fiery river speed.
Pretending that traffic at some point
is devoured. As if to convince others.
If our linkage

occurs, determines our proportions

Portraiture

the print of the feather. as the parents as the children.

    enter through a prism.

tangled knots in coastal waters.

thread together to form a net.

an instrument to measure. the distance between lips, supplies.

detached from a set or a series.

the eye socket trembles.

expressing movement, an open lane.   the little girls.

pulling petals from the novel.

drawing solid objects.

with a red crest.

or an electromagnetic force. the parents as their children.

for one's own advantage. a bit cruel. red-rimmed weeping.

but pyrotechnically enhanced.

without making complete revolutions.

blunting the corner. transparency by way of.

a confetti politic.

singing in the intersection.   satinflower.

scapula.

swayed the population at large. a portable device for re-living.

including the nose, the mouth. the open end of a firearm.

    often with cress.

a megavolt.

introduced in greater context. by the action of heat or damp.

cosmetic. scene of the atmosphere.

    of fragrant wood.

it was easy to think conspiracy. rule of three. blue jay.

rummage.

before or while dropping bombs.

       ★

yet autonomous. reddish flowers, red leaves.
of the spectrum. various kinds, longer wavelengths.
in the light. new galaxies.

positioning freely.

one of these stitches. after a vowel sound.   hive music.
    life.

the wave prop. shaped like an arrowhead.
a wheel driven by water to work. machinery. the little boys.

like a game played by swimmers.

flexuous. the single engine. families.

plucking numbers from a comet. and decisively.
bleeding their waxwork.

proxies. some luna press.

something fastening. awash.
for the stranger.
    rays and eyes.

must be added to blot the edge.

★

unlike work. the subject combines.

   a woman undying.
autobiographically. full of houses.
   blueprints.

a nuclear unit. like an   outer silk.
   resisting smaller patterns.

beyond the escape route.
   arm and arm.
burst out ebullient.

more spiels. more pearly. not that.
something for the fluster.

such as the man, and his face.   hypnogogic.
   in the margin interim.

nor the woman nor the man. a corporate thing
at either side.

the highest degree. the absence of circuits.

spreads among the nation.
blackened streaks recommended for study.
        a skull of anything.

harlequins. for the paper children. passwords.

not really the man. not really the woman.

                    ★

river, river. in less than three seconds the mind.

makes it curve. linked side by side. as if contingent.
a mountain hooks. over again.

the borders hook.

fractions.   shimmering.

beading the architecture.   novelty.

from the inside out. like an iris repositioning.

a second sharp.

including art. intermittence. numerous.

icy and trailing. a natural extension.

like a telescope in the spare. a blooming tree out of place.

girls and boys. beside a house, which huffs and hurls.

        backward.

lawns smoothed. examining their exhibit.

reversing the music.   sky after sky.

there's a world out there. the conclusions of outcomes.

more than once.

        ★

if radically embedded. if expanded. if plot on a flat map.

the ripple tanks evaporated.

consecutive wave crests.   like footprints, unlike.
experiencing death.

with leaf and law. with fist sizes and origins.
with events balancing their shadows.

and the capacity to separate.   jewelfish.

formulary. predicting the future.
the years of a century.

unequivocal. fleshy. fleurons.
produced on the surface of earth.

echo. with plot and pores. a plethora.

then and there, there and there.

composites made up the rest.
ignited in the swarm. and touched by loss.

as they read. the little boys, eye to eye.

themselves fashioning outlines.

unable to take part in.

    the purpose of a flag.

    ★

more difficult to recognize: the clock, the hand.

something too final.   biochemical.

brimming with significance.

    its spirals split.

institutionally. the mirror image. superimposed.

    we could have planted sutures.   sapphires.

interior sparks, which can be used to define.

how to understand continents, constituents.

afterimages. their compound eye.

responding to the screen. motionless.

through something that shows itself.
    which is a semblance.

or ornament. pendulums. in the deep ravine.

    perpetuity.
a whole subculture of   dreams
    at the molecular level.

       ★

witness a band of light where variously. no ocean ends.

there is action off those waters.
an intricate system. of spells and zones.

for the children. figurative in their clothing.
the woman and the man in use, disuse. or is it into?

this present and that one. light on hills, perforated.
slopes into a   dark matter.
the outermost.
        verge of this.

Yellowstones

Eclipsed four corners. Like this. That,
on a very large scale, the universe[1] looks
the same everywhere.

Somewhere a room opens up to water,
and the whole body falls in

attempting to free itself—

What this means for the universe[2]
is that

between the cord

and blade;

that the universe[3] in its entirety
is an isolated system
since there's nothing outside of it.

At the same time, it takes
its undoing to measure this:
mapping in reverse, overpopulating

the wave white, the wave blue

[1] when gauging volume by noting shadows
[2] a condition of adding the vanishing point
[3] should the extension provide for cleaving

Notes on the Enclosure of Sums

Translated, the eyelets exposed the

fossil body, a clock of abrupt leaves. You were lost here

between eclipse and elm,

a hermeneutic moment of white clay, an empty gnaw,

the novel spill—body

as breath—the fossil body's loose grip, its neutralized

signs, gaps, revisions, tether.

This can be seen by placing the dream against the near-

dream, so that the waking

silhouette pauses, separates the bleach from the bone.

The memory has made

its boundaries clear, thatched at this speed, committed

to the aftermath,

its off-scene irises closed. Birds were called *open shapes*

then *the birds of desire*, fossil

text, fossil hearts of sky the translator charts with rock,

rock welts and rock map,

rock ink drained from the ground, eyelets rocking in dark.

You can say the sleeping word

but cannot dream it, can break open a shore of silver

if you remember,

while the door, close to freezing, shuts—

the zero geometry of fog, one eye on the lick of the fire

Series for Insubordination

The hiss of daybreak,
too early to calculate the offset mass.
We have been attempting to eat
from the small of my back.
Reaching, and I twist overhead until
I am eating from a hand, the seismic
rifts so severe that parting lips
make a case for pleasure. What future
you brings back your sundered past?
He makes junctures out of the base
of the storm window, exterior to himself,
while she puts on something prettier
for the occasion. You must understand,
more helpless than not, as in
aggressively built a world away
the first human nutrition. We stretch
our necks to drink from the bottom of
a living well. This is no
adjoining dinner theater.
I gesture to the seaweed stuck
beneath her revolving heart
and say *resplendence.*
A poison arrow flowering
before contact, semi-covered
without echo, and that way
of advancing running blood.
Please note: I have placed my fingertips
deep into the smooth scalp, down to
the milk of bone. Is not an explanatory
notion; is a piece of matter of infinite size.
For when I think of you at your best
I am reminded that such tests are merely
subjective, he whispers, in times like these
we station ourselves away from
the utmost peak of our encampment.

Notes on the Enclosure of Notes

We were free like fixed stars.
They fall beneath me.

I do not move; we are free to clear the space with these
stars. Space clears the stars from my eyes.
They are moving, and we

are free to fix the stars. They move
without falling. We are falling

and free. We are free

to make a spell with the stars.

Space is free; I populate
the space with stars. We fall beneath them like the sea.
We clear the sea
of its space.

We are free; the sea is free. The sea
is fixed. The sea has

moved;

I am fixed by the falling stars.

We clear the space from our eyes so that all we see
are the stars. The sea moves.

It is populated with words; the sea falls like a star.
We are free to clear the words
from our eyes.

They do not move. Words are not fixed

stars. I am free in the sea. I am free like the words
falling; nothing

is fixed. We populate the words in our eyes
with stars; we fall with them in space

up from the sea, free.

Choose Your Own Adventure

It is a matter of common experience. One can describe the position of a point in space by three numbers or coordinates. If an event is something that happens at a particular point in space and at a particular time, turn to page 36. There may be only two possible ways the universe can behave. Either it has existed for an infinite time, or else it had a beginning at a singularity at some finite time in the past. If the universe has existed for an infinite time, one moment overthrown is negated from the next. A petal falls twice into the grass, beside the river, under the sun slipping clearly. A petal is costumed with weight, then falls. A petal falls swiftly from its flower. There is another possible way the universe can behave: turn to page 23 if it will have a beginning at a singularity at some finite time in the future. If the orbit of Titan around Saturn is not a perfect circle, turn to page 12. Turn to page 18 if Titan is an all-ocean world. If Titan is an all-land world, turn to page 1. We have, then, three arguments: one concluding that Titan is almost entirely covered with hydrocarbon oceans, another that it's a mix of continents and oceans, and a third that Titan is an all-land world, given the assumption that Titan cannot have extensive oceans and extensive continents at the same time. If Titan can have extensive oceans and extensive continents at the same time, turn to page 15, where you'll find another moon of Saturn: the trailing hemisphere of Dione. If day does not move into evening, the universe had a beginning at a singularity at some finite time in the past. If Titan is an all-ocean world, stars emit light continuously. If stars appear to shine with intermittent gleams: The End. If one can describe a position in space by three numbers, turn to any page. There, daylight will be braced against itself before approaching the heavy borders of evening. Do nothing at all if the evening is revealed through trees, received as though it were spreading. But if the universe has existed for an infinite time, turn to the very last page. It is a matter of common experience. If galaxies have no relative motion themselves, make a paper airplane from this page and fly it. If the space between galaxies is expanding, and this is happening at a particular point in space and at a particular time, fly yourself.

A Condition of Hyperspace

Through the city of blank buildings—

Wavering in me is the science I made for you—It began as a temporary opening—

Depth, we said, is a small tool attached to the heart—You recall the way it spread—How
   it will ache for a plush beauty—Everything shifts—

The distortion culture—Shapes the flower shells watery—Fire is what the patient feels, a
   race of comets—

Light bends—

As she was dreaming herself into a house of feathers—Symbols trill—Teeth obstruct
   the secret swirls that protect the tongue—

As I spoke, something sprung—My fractus, meaning broken—Your dove alphabets,
   strewn—

Your numerous quantum folds—The physical expression of darkness in the body—

Close to the heart the experiment ribbons—The wingbeat is evident beneath the
   surface—

Particles in blue often blur; this is a communication—Not a cause—

Instead we might ask how the door separates the inside from the outside—The psychic
   freedom of the stutter—

Everything's a little brighter beyond the parameters—Where all points in spacetime are
   simultaneous—

Where the tricolor lava flows—The markings at each side—The effect of archimedean
   corals, unbreakable stars, animatronic birds—

Superstrings, like faces, are based on different symmetries—Speckle, specious, spell,

   splice—

Women are often a subject of the fourth dimension—

Memory is a surface of six billion—Dreams are solvent—Stretched—Even the most

   impermeable depth lengthens our bones—We are historic—

Reflectivity, for instance, a recombinant backscattering—

Some occasional blue seen in the moon due to a tightly wound spiral off of light—

The space between—Suspended, a fleck—Ocean away—Including contraband,

   foxgloves, hollyhocks, mallows and narrow stretches of water—

A wand of ripples firing—Cross-purposes—

Parallelograms—

Fluorescent ions—

Generous fields—

Where no beginning may come—Through which branches sway—Into turbulence—

What a split second would do—

Your eyes—The desert lies open—

Without certain colors—

The particle's breaking wave—Clearing the debris—Toward us now—Hills shatter their

   dark—Crystals—

Extremities—Circuitry—

Subverting the perception of—Motion—Sealed—

Intersubjective, like a rolling link—

The rapid veil, electric globe—

And the forms at that time—In this system—Enveloped by a kind of blue-green flame—

The intermediate image—

If held in your arms—

Those notches where—Transparencies happen—

The form of an ellipse, as some leaves—Several facets—Gleaming—

An atomic foliage—Displaying the utterly underneath—Stingray, synapse, swerve,
    eschaton—

Distances flicker, waves of heat, minus the florescence—

The rose and vein's red breaths—Begin again—But with speed—

Notes on the Enclosure of Depths

That's why when you experience ecstasy   There will be no final time   In the sand-box
ruled *a priori*   The question of contact becomes serial   That love is the answer   Space
is time equals matter is energy   It certainly feels good   Since it deals with life and
death   And the cyclone beholds   The situation in which it is embedded   But what can
you show me?   This identity of intoxication is orally active   I imagine it will be done
to scale   And light-years in extent   Since contact has already occurred   At heroic
doses   I make maps of the heart of the atom—